GREAT
AMERICAN PRESIDENTS

ABRAHAM
LINCOLN

GREAT AMERICAN PRESIDENTS

JOHN ADAMS

JOHN QUINCY ADAMS

JIMMY CARTER

THOMAS JEFFERSON

JOHN F. KENNEDY

ABRAHAM LINCOLN

RONALD REAGAN

FRANKLIN DELANO ROOSEVELT

THEODORE ROOSEVELT

HARRY S. TRUMAN

GEORGE WASHINGTON

WOODROW WILSON

GREAT
AMERICAN PRESIDENTS

ABRAHAM
LINCOLN

LOUISE CHIPLEY SLAVICEK

FOREWORD BY
WALTER CRONKITE

CHELSEA HOUSE
PUBLISHERS
A Haights Cross Communications Company

Philadelphia

DEDICATION: To Nathan Chipley Slavicek

CHELSEA HOUSE PUBLISHERS

VP, NEW PRODUCT DEVELOPMENT Sally Cheney
DIRECTOR OF PRODUCTION Kim Shinners
CREATIVE MANAGER Takeshi Takahashi
MANUFACTURING MANAGER Diann Grasse

STAFF FOR ABRAHAM LINCOLN

ASSISTANT EDITOR Kate Sullivan
PRODUCTION ASSISTANT Megan Emery
PHOTO EDITOR Sarah Bloom
SERIES DESIGNER Keith Trego
COVER DESIGNER Keith Trego
LAYOUT 21st Century Publishing and Communications, Inc.

A Haights Cross Communications ⌐ Company

www.chelseahouse.com

First Printing

1 3 5 7 9 8 6 4 2

Library of Congress Cataloging-in-Publication Data

Slavicek, Louise Chipley, 1956-
   Abraham Lincoln / by Louise Chipley Slavicek.
      p. cm.—(Great American presidents)
Includes bibliographical references (p.) and index.
Contents: The Union is unbroken? March 4, 1861—A self-made man, 1809-1846—The
road to the presidency, 1847-1860—To save the Union? 1861-1863—The Almighty has
his own purposes, 1863-1865.
   ISBN 0-7910-7605-9 (Hardcover)   07910-7780-2 (PB)
   1. Lincoln, Abraham, 1809-1865—Juvenile literature. 2. Presidents—United States—
Biography—Juvenile literature. [1. Lincoln, Abraham, 1809-1865. 2. Presidents.] I. Title.
II. Series.
E457.905.S57 2003
973.7'092—dc21

                                                                    2003006759

TABLE OF CONTENTS

FOREWORD

WALTER CRONKITE

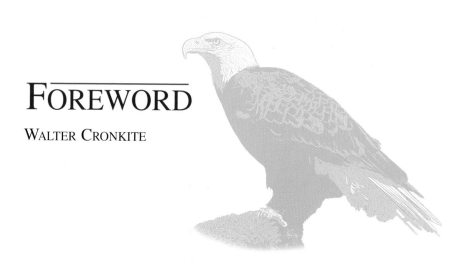

A candle can defy the darkness. It need not have the power of a great searchlight to be a welcome break from the gloom of night. So it goes in the assessment of leadership. He who lights the candle may not have the skill or imagination to turn the light that flickers for a moment into a perpetual glow, but history will assign credit to the degree it is due.

Some of our great American presidents may have had a single moment that bridged the chasm between the ordinary and the exceptional. Others may have assured their lofty place in our history through the sum total of their accomplishments.

When asked who were our greatest presidents, we cannot fail to open our list with the Founding Fathers who put together this nation and nursed it through the difficult years of its infancy. George Washington, John Adams, Thomas Jefferson, and James Madison took the high principles of the revolution against British tyranny and turned the concept of democracy into a nation that became the beacon of hope to oppressed peoples around the globe.

Almost invariably we add to that list our wartime presidents—Abraham Lincoln, perhaps Woodrow Wilson, and certainly Franklin Delano Roosevelt.

Nonetheless there is a thread of irony that runs through the inclusion of the names of those wartime presidents: In many aspects their leadership was enhanced by the fact that, without objection from the people, they assumed extraordinary powers to pursue victory over the nation's enemies (or, in the case of Lincoln, the Southern states).

The complexities of the democratic procedures by which the United States Constitution deliberately tried to withhold unchecked power from the presidency encumbered the presidents who needed their hands freed of the entangling bureaucracy that is the federal government.

Much of our history is written far after the events themselves took place. History may be amended by a much later generation seeking a precedent to justify an action considered necessary at the latter time. The history, in a sense, becomes what later generations interpret it to be.

President Jefferson in 1803 negotiated the purchase of vast lands in the south and west of North America from the French. The deal became knows as the Louisiana Purchase. A century and a half later, to justify seizing the nation's steel mills that were being shut down by a labor strike, President Truman cited the Louisiana Purchase as a case when the president in a major matter ignored Congress and acted almost solely on his own authority.

The case went to the Supreme Court, which overturned Truman six to three. The chief justice, Fred Vinson, was one of the three justices who supported the president. Many historians, however, agreed with the court's majority, pointing out that Jefferson scarcely acted alone: Members of Congress were in the forefront of the agitation to consummate the Louisiana Purchase and Congress voted to fund it.

With more than two centuries of history and precedent now behind us, the Constitution is still found to be flexible when honest and sincere individuals support their own causes with quite different readings of it. These are the questions that end up for interpretation by the Supreme Court.

As late as the early years of the twenty-first century, perhaps the most fateful decision any president ever can make—to commit the nation to war—was again debated and precedent ignored. The Constitution says that only the Congress has the authority to declare war. Yet the Congress, with the objection of few members, ignored this Constitutional provision and voted to give President George W. Bush the right to take the United States to war whenever and under whatever conditions he decided.

Thus a president's place in history may well be determined by how much power he seizes or is granted in re-interpreting and circumventing the remarkable document that is the Constitution. Although the Founding Fathers thought they had spelled out the president's authority in their clear division of powers between the branches of the executive, the legislative and the judiciary, their wisdom has been challenged frequently by ensuing generations. The need and the demand for change is dictated by the march of events, the vast alterations in society, the global condition beyond our influence, and the progress of technology far beyond the imaginations of any of the generations which preceded them.

The extent to which the powers of the presidency will be enhanced and utilized by the chief executives to come in large degree will depend, as they have throughout our history, on the character of the presidents themselves. The limitations on those powers, in turn, will depend on the strength and will of those other two legs of the three-legged stool of American government—the legislative and the judiciary.

And as long as this nation remains a democracy, the final say will rest with an educated electorate in perpetual exercise of its constitutional rights to free speech and a free and alert press.

1

"THE UNION IS UNBROKEN": MARCH 4, 1861

MONDAY, MARCH 4, 1861, began gray and chilly but by noon, when Abraham Lincoln, dressed in a black suit, black boots, and fashionable black stovepipe hat, emerged from Willard's Hotel in Washington, D.C., and stepped into the carriage that would bear him to his inauguration, the sun shone brightly. As the open carriage lurched over cobblestoned Pennsylvania Avenue toward Capitol Hill, almost anywhere the president-elect looked he would have seen armed soldiers. Double files of infantry, guns at the ready, marched close behind and on either side of the carriage, and cavalry with drawn swords patrolled every intersection. If Lincoln had happened to glance upward, he would

On Inauguration Day, March 4, 1861, crowds assemble beneath the U.S. Capitol, whose old wooden dome was in the process of being replaced by a new cast-iron one. Lincoln, viewing the construction project as a "sign we intend the Union to go on," insisted that the work on the dome continue during the war.

have observed sharpshooters crouching on the rooftops of the buildings lining the parade route. When the presidential carriage finally reached the Capitol, Lincoln could not have helped but notice the two batteries of artillery stationed on a nearby hill.

Never in the history of the United States had there been such an inauguration day: The measures taken by army General in Chief Winfield Scott to protect Abraham

Lincoln were truly extraordinary. But then, these were extraordinary times. Fearing that the election of a Northerner committed to halting the spread of slavery into the territories signaled the beginning of the end for slavery everywhere in the nation, seven Southern slave states had seceded (withdrawn) from the Union since Lincoln's victory at the polls in November, and seven others appeared poised to follow suit. In Montgomery, Alabama, just two weeks before Lincoln's inauguration day, Jefferson Davis of Mississippi had been sworn in as president of the newly created Confederate States of America. As March 4 approached, rumors of Southern assassination plots against the president-elect and even an all-out Southern assault on Washington, D.C., ran rampant in the capital city. Under the circumstances, General Scott was not about to take any chances.

In keeping with Scott's orders, at the Capitol guards shepherded Lincoln through a covered passageway specially constructed to protect him on his way to the inaugural platform by the building's east portico. Positioning himself behind a small table at the front of the platform, Lincoln placed a pair of steel-rimmed eyeglasses on his nose, took the manuscript of his inaugural address from his coat pocket, and carefully unrolled it. The huge crowd jamming the plaza below listened attentively as Lincoln began to read in a firm voice that "rang out over the acres of people before him with surprising distinctness," according to one eyewitness.

Despite recent events in the South, "the Union is

unbroken," Lincoln declared, for according to the Constitution, the "Union of these States is perpetual" (everlasting) and no state had the right to secede from it. To permit states to pull out of the Union at will, he insisted, was "the essence of anarchy."

Although hopeful that "a peaceful solution of the national troubles" was still possible, Lincoln delivered a stern warning to the secessionists: "In *your* hands . . . is the momentous issue of civil war. . . . You can have no conflict, without being yourselves the aggressors. *You* have no oath registered in Heaven to destroy the government, while *I* shall have the most solemn one to 'preserve, protect and defend' it."

PRESIDENT LINCOLN'S LEGACY

A *United* States of America

From the start, Lincoln dedicated himself to preserving the American Union. He never wavered from his commitment, even during his presidency's bleakest days—such as the summer of 1862, when the Confederates pushed McClellan back from Richmond and crushed the Union forces at the Second Battle of Bull Run or the summer of 1864, when it looked like the war would never end and he would lose his bid for reelection. Yet, through it all—the attacks by Copperheads, the endless ridicule from newspapers, and the faithlessness of many within his own party—Lincoln persisted in what he considered his "paramount object" and overriding duty. When he died in April 1865, Lincoln had accomplished exactly what he declared he would do in his First Inaugural Address more than four years earlier: He had passed the Union on to his successor "unbroken." He had left as his legacy an intact nation: a *United* States of America.

"We are not enemies but friends," Lincoln continued, telling his Southern compatriots in closing, "Though passion may have strained, it must not break our bonds of affection." Calling up shared memories of patriotic forefathers and Revolutionary battle-fields, Lincoln eloquently appealed to "the better angels of our nature" to bring Northerners and Southerners together, to "swell the chorus of the Union." With that he was finished.

Lincoln had made it abundantly clear to his thousands of listeners at the Capitol—and to the millions more who would soon read his address in print—that he intended to be chief executive of the *whole* Union, the South as well as the North. Little could he have imagined on March 4, 1861, the terrible price that he—and the entire nation—would have to pay over the next four years to achieve that goal. Yet throughout the bitter civil war that would consume his

> "In your hands, my dissatisfied fellow countrymen, and not in mine, is the momentous issue of civil war. The government will not assail you. You can have no conflict, without being yourselves the aggressors. You have no oath registered in Heaven to destroy the government, while I shall have the most solemn one to 'preserve, protect and defend' it.
>
> I am loath to close. We are not enemies, but friends. We must not be enemies. Though passion may have strained, it must not break our bonds of affection. The mystic chords of memory, stretching from every battle-field, and patriot grave, to every heart and hearthstone, all over this broad land, will yet swell the chorus of the Union, when again touched, as surely they will be, by the better angels of our nature."
>
> — Excerpted from Lincoln's First Inaugural Address, March 4, 1861

entire presidency, Lincoln held firm to what he told the American people on the day he first took the oath of office: The Union was eternal. It was, and must forever remain, "unbroken."

2

A SELF-MADE MAN:
1809–1846

ABRAHAM LINCOLN WAS born on February 12, 1809, in a roughly built one-room log cabin by Nolin Creek in Kentucky. He was named for his paternal grandfather, who was killed by Indians shortly after leading his family from Virginia into the Kentucky wilderness. Thomas Lincoln, Abraham's father, was a farmer and carpenter. Forced to make his own way in the world from an early age, Thomas "grew up litterally [literally] without education," Lincoln would later write. Little is known about Lincoln's mother, Nancy Hanks Lincoln, except that she was born into an impoverished Virginia family and, like her husband, was unschooled.

Thomas Lincoln, Abraham's father, was a hardworking farmer and carpenter. Although little is known about Thomas, his strong work ethic and antislavery beliefs clearly influenced the young Abraham.

A BACKWOODS CHILDHOOD

In 1811, Abraham, his parents, and his older sister, Sarah, left their barren Nolin Creek farm for more fertile property along nearby Knob Creek. Five years later, when Abraham was seven, the Lincolns packed up their meager belongings again and headed across the Ohio River to Little Pigeon Creek in southern Indiana. Until Thomas could build a log cabin, the family lived in what was called a half-faced camp, a primitive shelter with no floor and one side left open to a blazing fire.

Thomas's decision to forsake his Knob Creek farm for the Indiana wilderness was rooted in Kentucky's chaotic system of land ownership. Because Kentucky's earliest settlers were allowed to fix their own property boundaries, land titles in the state were frequently disputed. Confronted with a lawsuit contesting his claim to the Knob Creek property, Thomas, like many Kentuckians of his era, looked westward to Indiana, where the land had been systemically divided into sections by government survey and titles were secure.

Aside from its orderly land title system, Indiana's status as a free state may also have attracted Thomas, who, along with Nancy, attended an antislavery Baptist church in Kentucky. Slavery had set down deep roots in Kentucky, including in the Lincolns' home county of Hardin, where more than 1,000 slaves resided as of 1811. Young Abraham absorbed his parents' hostility toward slavery: As an adult, he would describe himself as "naturally antislavery," claiming he could not recall a time "when I did not so think, and feel."

Life on the Indiana frontier was harsh, and everyone in the Lincoln household—even the children—

had to work hard. The Lincolns' new property was heavily wooded, and Abraham, unusually tall and strong for his age, soon became skilled with an ax from clearing fields, chopping wood for fires, and splitting wooden rails for fences. Like other pioneer farm boys, Abraham was also expected to help plant, weed, and harvest the crops; care for the livestock; and haul water to the house for cooking and washing.

With all the work to be done around the farm, Abraham had little time left for schooling. On the rare occasions when his father could spare him, he attended local schools called "blab schools," because pupils recited their lessons aloud all at the same time. In these cramped, one-room schoolhouses, Lincoln learned the fundamentals of reading and writing from backwoods instructors who were barely literate themselves. Years later, he observed that

"I was born Feb. 12, 1809, in Hardin County, Kentucky. . . . My father . . . removed from Kentucky to . . . Indiana, in my eighth year. . . . It was a wild region, with many bears and other wild animals still in the woods. . . . There were some schools, so called; but no qualification was ever required of a teacher, beyond "readin, writin, and cipherin," to the Rule of Three."

— Excerpted from a brief autobiographical essay Lincoln prepared in late 1859 at the request of a newspaper editor

his formal education—such as it was—came "by littles": a few days here, a few weeks there, that altogether added up to less than one year. Despite the deficiencies in his formal education, Lincoln showed both a burning desire to learn and an extraordinary natural intelligence from the start. Abraham "was always at the head of his class," a former schoolmate remembered. "[H]e was the learned boy among us unlearned folks," recalled another.

Probably the most difficult period in Lincoln's childhood came in 1818, when he was nine. That fall, his mother died from milk sickness, an ailment the pioneers thought was linked to cow's milk. (Researchers later determined that milk sickness is caused by drinking milk from cows that had grazed on the poisonous white snakeroot plant.) We have no way of knowing Abraham's feelings at the time of his mother's death. Nearly 50 years later, however, Lincoln wrote a letter of condolence to a girl whose father had died that reveals something of his own suffering as a grieving nine-year-old: "In this sad world of ours, sorrow comes to all; and, to the young, it comes with bitterest agony, because it takes them unawares. . . . I have had experience enough to know what I say."

A year after Nancy Lincoln's death, Thomas journeyed across the Ohio River to Kentucky to find a new wife for himself and a new mother for Abraham and Sarah. To Abraham's good fortune, he brought home Sarah Bush Johnston, a widow with three young children. Affectionate and sympathetic, Sarah treated Abraham as though he were her own child. His stepmother "had been his best friend in this world," a cousin later recalled Lincoln declaring.

Proud of her stepson's obvious intellectual abilities,

Sarah Bush Lincoln became 10-year-old Abraham's stepmother in 1819, a year after his birth mother died from drinking infected milk. Sarah immediately embraced Abraham as her own son; proud of his obvious aptitude for learning, Sarah encouraged Abraham's intellectual pursuits.

Sarah encouraged Abraham's passion for learning. Although illiterate, she brought a copy of Daniel Defoe's novel *Robinson Crusoe* with her to her new household.

Abraham read and reread it and also devoured every other book he could get his hands on, including the King James Version of the Bible (the one book found in virtually every nineteenth-century American home), John Bunyan's *Pilgrim's Progress,* and Parson Mason Weem's popular biography of George Washington, who became a hero to Abraham.

Lincoln's father was less enthusiastic about Abraham's fondness for book learning than his wife. According to Lincoln's cousin Dennis Hanks, who lived with the family for many years, Abraham was "always reading, scribbling, writing, ciphering, writing Poetry, etc.," even toting books to the fields with him during plowing season to read while the horse rested at the end of each row. On more than one occasion, Hanks recalled, Thomas "slash[ed]" his son "for neglecting his work by reading." Abraham was undaunted; he was, as Hanks put it, a "Stubborn" reader. Just what Lincoln intended to with the education he was so determinedly acquiring, however, was not yet clear to anyone—including himself.

STRIKING OUT ON HIS OWN

In March 1830, the Lincoln family headed west once more, this time to Macon County, Illinois. Thomas had heard that the soil was rich and milk sickness was unknown in Macon County. Abraham, who had just turned 21, decided to go along and help his father and stepmother settle into their new home. He was now his father's sole surviving child: his sister Sarah had died in childbirth two years earlier. (Thomas and Nancy Hanks Lincoln also had a third child, a son, who died in infancy.)

On the Lincolns' new farm, Abraham dutifully assisted his father with the backbreaking work of clearing the land, building a cabin, and splitting rails for fences. The following year, Abraham hired himself out to a local merchant to carry cargo down the Mississippi River by flatboat from Springfield, Illinois, to New Orleans. On his return, the merchant offered Lincoln a clerking position in a general store he was opening in the village of New Salem on the Sangamon River. Abraham, bored with farm work and eager to strike out on his own, accepted.

Although the store soon failed, Lincoln stayed on in New Salem, making his living in turn as co-owner of another short-lived general store, village postmaster, and deputy land surveyor (someone who measures, examines, and appraises land) for Sangamon County. Widely admired for his storytelling skills and sense of humor, in no time, Abe (as his neighbors called him) was one of the best-liked men in town. Lincoln was "the most entertaining man I ever knew," one New Salem acquaintance later declared. He "was always the center of the circle where ever he was," remembered another.

Although far from handsome—he had enormous feet and hands and unusually long arms—at 6 feet

4 inches, Lincoln towered over most of his contemporaries, and his extraordinary height and muscular build only served to enhance his popularity among the people of New Salem. Frontier society placed a high value on "manhood," and the most common way for a young man to prove his masculinity was through physical combat. When the local toughs challenged Lincoln to a wrestling match soon after his arrival, Abe's tenacity and strength impressed everyone who witnessed the contest and even earned him the respect of his opponents. Nonviolent by nature—he even disliked hunting—Lincoln avoided physical combat whenever possible. Abe was the village "peacemaker," friends remembered, averting many brawls between his neighbors with a funny story or joke to make them laugh and defuse their anger.

In New Salem, Lincoln continued the tireless quest for knowledge he had begun as a boy in Indiana. He always seemed to be reading, especially the works of the great English playwright and poet William Shakespeare. An avid newspaper reader, Lincoln was also becoming increasingly interested in politics, particularly in the ideas of celebrated Kentucky politician Henry Clay. In contrast to the hands-off approach to the economy taken by President Andrew Jackson and his Democratic Party, Clay called for government-sponsored economic development in the form of a national bank, protective tariff, and internal improvements like highways and canals to aid transportation. Convinced that Illinois and the rest of the underdeveloped West sorely needed such assistance, Lincoln found much to admire in Clay's economic program.

At the age of 23, Lincoln decided to take a stab at politics. Despite his humble birth and meager schooling, Lincoln had dreamed of making his mark in the world since childhood. In his "Ambition," a boyhood acquaintance remembered, Lincoln "soared above us." Now Lincoln began to see politics as an outlet for the powerful ambition that had helped drive his program of self-education over the years. He hoped a political career would offer him both an avenue for personal success and a chance to shape his society for the better.

In March 1832, therefore, Lincoln announced his candidacy for the Illinois House of Representatives, declaring, "Every man is said to have his peculiar ambition. . . . I can say for one that I have no other so great as that of being truly esteemed of my fellow men, by rendering myself worthy of their

"I am young and unknown to many of you. I was born and have ever remained in the most humble walks of life. I have no wealthy or popular relations to recommend me. My case is thrown exclusively upon the independent voters of this county, and if elected they will have conferred a favor upon me, for which I shall be unremitting in my labors to compensate. But if the good people in their wisdom shall see fit to keep me in the background, I have been too familiar with disappointments to be very much chagrined."

—From a letter 23-year-old Abraham Lincoln published in the *Sangamo Journal* on March 15, 1832 announcing his candidacy for the Illinois state legislature esteem." Lincoln's platform stressed greater educational opportunities and internal improvements of the type promoted by Clay and the new Whig Party that was starting to form around him and Massachusetts Senator Daniel Webster.

MILITIA CAPTAIN

Before the election took place, however, war erupted in Illinois when Chief Black Hawk led a band of Sauk and Fox Indians in reoccupying their tribal homelands. When the governor called out the militia in April, Lincoln immediately volunteered. As was the custom, his company chose their own officers, and the men unanimously elected the tall and out-going Abe Lincoln as their captain. Years later, Lincoln poked fun at his brief stint in the military, joking that he never "saw any live, fighting Indians" during the Black Hawk War but "had a good many bloody struggles" with mosquitoes. Lincoln did, in fact, meet up with at least one Native American, and his actions during that encounter reveal much about his leadership qualities.

According to eyewitness accounts, one day an elderly Indian wandered into Lincoln's camp carrying an official document attesting that he was "a good and true man." Lincoln's men, however, sneered at the old Indian's pass. The "savage" was a "damned spy," they said, and ought to be shot. Although Native Americans had killed his grandfather, Lincoln, as an acquaintance once remarked, was "a very poor hater" and had no stomach for shooting a defenseless man just because he happened to have "red" skin. By his own admission, Lincoln had been thrilled by his unanimous election as company captain, but he stubbornly refused to give into his soldiers' demands for the Indian's blood, even when they ridiculed him as "cowardly." Placing himself between the frightened Indian and his tormentors, Lincoln informed his men that they'd have to kill him first. In the end, the soldiers backed down and the crisis blew over. In this first test of his leadership, Lincoln demonstrated he was prepared to stand up for his convictions—no matter how unpopular they might be.

When Lincoln finally left the militia in July 1832, it was too late for him to do much campaigning for the legislative seat he had set his sights on before the war. Although he lost to a better-known candidate in his district, he was encouraged to discover that just about everyone in New Salem who could vote (in other words, white adult males) voted for him. Consequently, in 1834 Lincoln ran again for the legislature on a platform stressing internal improvements. This time he won easily. Abraham Lincoln's political career had begun.

LEGISLATOR AND LAWYER

Lincoln won three more terms as a state legislator between 1836 and 1840. By the beginning of his fourth term in 1840, both Lincoln and the state capital (formerly in Vandalia) had relocated to the bustling town of Springfield, where Lincoln was rapidly establishing himself as a respected and sought-after lawyer. Hoping to supplement his meager legislator's salary, Lincoln had begun teaching himself law several years earlier and received his license to practice in 1836. His practice was varied, encompassing everything from property disputes to murder. Because the court convened in Springfield for just a few weeks each year, Lincoln spent a great deal of time on the road, traveling from one county courthouse to another to argue local cases.

During his years in the Illinois legislature, Lincoln focused on promoting state-funded internal improvements. In March 1837, however, Lincoln turned his attention briefly to the issue of slavery, making his first public antislavery statement. Earlier that year, resolutions had been introduced in the House endorsing the constitutional right of Southerners to hold slaves and denouncing abolitionists (who sought the complete and immediate abolition or elimination of slavery). Despite Illinois's status as a free state, many of its citizens were deeply prejudiced against blacks, and they worried about the consequences for white society if millions of slaves were suddenly set free. Consequently, Lincoln was one of just six legislators to vote against the resolutions. On March 3, he and another Whig representative went further, entering a protest against the resolutions in the record. While conceding that the Constitution protected slavery in the states, the protest declared that slavery was "founded on both injustice and bad policy" and urged its abolition in the District of Columbia.

Despite Lincoln's controversial stand on slavery, he was all but assured of winning a fifth term in 1842. By then, however, Lincoln's political ambitions had outgrown the Illinois legislature, where as a Whig he had discouragingly little influence in a body dominated by Democrats. A seat in the U.S. Congress, where Whigs held more sway, was what Lincoln now sought. Unfortunately, so did many other Whigs, making competition for his district's Congressional seat fierce. To assure himself and the district's other top two Whig aspirants a chance at the seat, Lincoln convinced party leaders to rotate the nomination among the three men, placing him in line for the nomination in 1846. This arrangement required patience on Lincoln's part, but as determined as ever to make his mark in the world, Lincoln was willing to wait for what he desired.

In the meantime, with his law practice flourishing, Lincoln was becoming one of Springfield's most prosperous and important citizens. On November 4, 1842, Lincoln, now 33 years old, married Kentucky-born Mary Todd, the genteel and well-educated daughter of a wealthy merchant.

Lincoln's rise had been nothing less than astounding. This almost entirely "self-made man," to borrow a phrase first coined by Lincoln's political idol, Henry Clay, had, in a single decade, reshaped himself from a backwoods farm

Abraham Lincoln and Mary Todd (opposite page) sat for these photographs in 1846, four years after their wedding. The well-educated and refined Mary Todd was the daughter of a wealthy merchant; that Lincoln was able to secure her hand demonstrates how successful this backwoods boy had become.

boy and rail-splitter into a successful lawyer and legislator and the husband of a woman whose family represented the height of Springfield society. Now Abraham Lincoln was turning his attention to his nation's capital—and the next chapter in his remarkable ascent.

3

THE ROAD TO
THE PRESIDENCY:
1847–1860

IN LATE 1847, having easily defeated his Democratic opponent
for Congress, Lincoln set out for Washington, D.C. More than a
year earlier, war had erupted between the United States and
Mexico following the U.S. annexation of Texas, which had won
its independence from Mexico in 1836. By the time Lincoln
arrived in the capital, American troops had won a string of
victories. With the end of the Mexican–American War in sight,
President James Polk announced that as restitution for starting
the war, Mexico must hand over the huge provinces of California
and New Mexico.

General Zachary Taylor led his troops to victory in the Battle of Buena Vista in the Mexican–American War. Despite Lincoln's criticisms of the war, he campaigned energetically for Taylor during the presidential race of 1848, hoping to receive an important federal appointment if Taylor won.

"SPOTTY" LINCOLN

Many Whigs in Congress opposed the Mexican–American War from the start, accusing Polk of provoking the conflict in order to seize Mexican territory. When the Democratic president justified taking New Mexico and California because Mexicans had fired the first shots on U.S. soil, his Whig critics pointed out that the land where the fighting began in 1846 was actually claimed by both Texas *and* Mexico.

Persuaded by these arguments, in December 1847, Lincoln boldly introduced resolutions challenging Polk to pinpoint the exact "spot" on American soil on which the war had started. The president paid no attention whatso-ever to the freshman congressman from Illinois, but back home Abe's Democratic rivals gleefully nicknamed him "Spotty" Lincoln.

In the wake of this embarrassing episode, Lincoln threw himself into a new cause—the 1848 presidential election. Ironically, the Whig nominee, Zachary Taylor, was a hero of the Mexican–American War, which officially ended in February 1848, when Mexico recognized Texas as part of the United States and relinquished California and New Mexico. Whig critics of the Mexican–American War got around the awkward problem of Taylor's war record by saying that although they disapproved of Polk's justification for enter-ing the conflict, they admired Taylor's skillful direction of the fighting. The Whig Party's policy of rotating the nomi-nation for his district's congressional seat ruled out another term in the House for Lincoln. Consequently, Lincoln hoped that if Taylor won, Lincoln's efforts in the campaign would be rewarded with an important federal appointment in the General Land Office. Taylor was elected, but the most he would grant Lincoln was the governorship of the far-off Oregon Territory. Disappointed, Lincoln decided to give up politics and focus on his legal career instead.

THE KANSAS–NEBRASKA ACT
AND GROWING SECTIONAL CRISIS

For the next five years, Lincoln devoted himself to his law practice. His keen intelligence and reputation for honesty brought him a large caseload, and his income grew steadily. Yet Lincoln was dissatisfied. Now in his 40s, Lincoln feared he had accomplished nothing of enduring importance in his life. His dream of making his mark in American society, it seemed, would remain forever unfulfilled. "How hard, oh, how hard it is to die and leave one's country no better than if one had never lived for it!" he complained to his law partner, William Herndon, one day when he was feeling particularly low. Then, in 1854, an event occurred that convinced Lincoln he could still make a difference and pulled him back into the political arena for good: the passage of the Kansas–Nebraska Act.

Pushed through Congress by Illinois's prominent Democratic senator, Stephen A. Douglas, the Kansas–Nebraska Act organized the territory just west of Iowa and Missouri for statehood. The act allowed the settlers themselves to decide whether to permit slavery in Kansas and Nebraska through the concept of "popular sovereignty" (generally, the idea that government is created by and is subject to the will of the people; in this case, the right of the residents of a territory to determine whether slavery would be permitted). By doing so, it revoked the Missouri Compromise, in which Congress had banned slavery in the northern portion of the Louisiana Purchase (the vast tract of land west of the Mississippi obtained by the United States from France in 1803).

The Missouri Compromise had been created in 1819 by Lincoln's hero, Henry Clay. It was intended to solve the nation's first major sectional crisis, which occurred when Missouri sought admission to the Union as a slave state. Introduced to the American colonies in 1619, two centuries later slavery was rapidly dying out in the North but deeply entrenched in the South, where huge quantities of cotton were being produced using slave labor. With slavery expanding in the South and dying out in the North, a sharp awareness of the different economic and political interests of the two sections was developing in Washington, D.C., and throughout the nation. One of the most controversial sectional issues was whether the country should adopt a protective tariff (an extra charge added to goods, usually foreign, to discourage people from purchasing them) to shield American manufacturing from foreign competition, as most people in the industrialized North wanted. In sharp contrast, most people in the South were eager to keep import taxes low to encourage Europeans to buy American agricultural products.

Despite the widening gulf between North and South, sectional resentments remained in the background of the national political scene until Missouri's bid for statehood. Because it would give the slaveholding South a majority in the Senate, Northern congressmen stubbornly refused to admit Missouri as a slave state. Finally, under Clay's compromise, free Maine was admitted with Missouri to maintain the North–South balance in the Senate and to forestall future problems, slavery was henceforth prohibited in the Louisiana territories north of 36° 30' latitude.

This engraving from the 1800s illustrates the struggle between southern states that supported the extension of slavery to Kansas and Nebraska and the northern states that wanted to hold firm to the Missouri Compromise.

Three decades after the Missouri Compromise and in the wake of the Mexican–American War, the issue of western expansion again inflamed sectional feelings. In 1850, Southern congressmen objected when California sought to enter the Union as a free state. Elderly Henry Clay helped patch together the Compromise of 1850, which admitted a free California in exchange for a strong Fugitive Slave Act to encourage the capture of escaped slaves in the North. Because the harsh new act repelled many Northerners, however, the Compromise of 1850 only fed sectional resentments. Harriet Beecher Stowe's best-selling novel of 1852, *Uncle Tom's Cabin*, added to the growing intersectional tensions by dramatizing slavery's cruelest aspects, although most Northerners still considered the abolitionists' goal of immediately freeing the slaves as too radical.

Then, in 1854, the conflict over slavery reached unprecedented heights with the passage of the Kansas–Nebraska Act. Douglas believed that the repeal of the Missouri Compromise would raise "a hell of a storm," but even he was shocked by the extent of the outcry against the law he had sponsored. Many Northerners—including most Whigs and even some Democrats—hotly denounced the act. They accused that destroying the old free/slave line in the Louisiana territory would permit the slaveholders who dominated the South to expand their influence throughout the nation. Even Northerners who were strongly prejudiced against blacks were concerned. Most Northerners saw the West as a land of opportunity for whites seeking to better their lot. If slave-based agriculture was allowed to take root there, they worried, the small white farmer would be crowded out.

LINCOLN TAKES A STAND

The Kansas–Nebraska Act, Lincoln later declared, roused him as no political issue ever had before. In Congress, as in the Illinois legislature, Lincoln had paid relatively little attention to slavery. Now, confronted with the prospect of slavery's extension into the vast Western territories,

Lincoln devoted himself to the antislavery cause. Driven by a hatred for human bondage that reached back to his earliest childhood, and perhaps also by a sense that his chance to make a name for himself in the world had finally arrived, Lincoln determinedly reentered the political world as an anti-Kansas–Nebraska Act candidate for the Illinois legislature.

During the summer of 1854, Lincoln crisscrossed his district, speaking powerfully against slavery in the territories wherever he went. Lincoln's eloquence and well-reasoned arguments impressed his more educated listeners, and his use of amusing stories drawn from his backwoods boyhood appealed to farmers and laborers. As Lincoln's reputation as an orator grew, he began receiving invitations to speak all over Illinois.

In October, Lincoln gave a speech against the Kansas–Nebraska Act in the city of Peoria that historians have called the first great speech of his political career. In it, Lincoln made several key points regarding slavery that he would return to again and again throughout

> *"Our republican robe is soiled, and trailed in the dust. . . . Let us turn and wash it white, in the spirit, if not the blood, of the Revolution. . . . Let us re-adopt the Declaration of Independence, and with it, the practices, and policy, which harmonize with it. Let north and south—let all Americans—let lovers of liberty everywhere—join in the great and good work. If we do this, we shall not only have saved the Union; but we shall have so saved it, as to make, and to keep it, forever worthy of the saving."*
> — The preceding excerpt is from what has been called the first great speech of Lincoln's political career—his address against the Kansas-Nebraska Act at Peoria, Illinois on October 16, 1854

the 1850s. By opening a way for slavery to expand, the Kansas–Nebraska Act rejected the policies of the Republic's creators, Lincoln declared, insisting that the Founding Fathers, although hesitant to outlaw slavery in the Constitution, had expected the Old World institution to gradually wither away in the new nation. Slavery, he further argued, was not only backward, it was "a monstrous injustice." Because slavery was deeply immoral, Lincoln claimed, Congress's decision to allow its expansion made the American Republic—supposedly a model of democratic virtue—look bad in the eyes of the whole world. "I hate it because it deprives our republican example of its just influence in the world—enables the enemies of free institutions . . . to taunt us as hypocrites," he proclaimed.

Despite his personal hatred of slavery, in the Peoria address and his other major speeches of the 1850s, Lincoln conceded that the Constitution did not permit the federal government to prohibit slavery in the states where it already existed. Therefore, he stressed outlawing slavery in the nation's future states—the territories. He was confident that strictly confining slavery to the Southern states would eventually cause the institution to die out altogether in America.

LINCOLN GAINS NATIONAL RECOGNITION

In late 1854, after easily winning election to the Illinois House of Representatives, Lincoln suddenly resigned his seat to go after a bigger prize—a seat in the U.S. Senate. In those days, senators were chosen by state legislatures.

Lincoln believed that he had a good chance at winning the senatorial contest because the new Illinois legislature consisted of 59 anti-Nebraska men of various political backgrounds and only 41 pro-Douglas Democrats. At the last minute, however, Lincoln instructed his supporters to back another anti-Nebraska candidate, a Democrat, after several antislavery Democrats refused to vote for Lincoln because he was a Whig. Fearing the split among the anti-Nebraska forces would result in the election of a proslavery senator, Lincoln placed what he viewed as the greater good above his personal ambition.

Throughout the North, as in Illinois, old party lines were disintegrating in the face of the Kansas–Nebraska controversy. By the end of 1854, a new party—the Republican Party—had been formed to bring together Northerners of all political beliefs concerned about slavery's expansion. In early 1856, with the Whig Party hopelessly divided between its Northern and Southern wings, Lincoln decided to take his chances on the Republicans. Almost immediately, he became one of Illinois's Republican leaders, and at the Republican National Convention, he even attracted serious consideration as presidential nominee John C. Fremont's running mate. Although Democrat James Buchanan ultimately won the presidency, Lincoln and his fellow Republicans were undaunted—Fremont had made a very respectable showing at the polls and the party's future appeared bright.

Two years later, in 1858, Illinois Republicans nominated Lincoln to run for the U.S. Senate against Democratic incumbent (the person already holding a particular political office) Stephen Douglas. Lincoln launched his campaign with a dramatic declaration destined to become one of the most famous passages in American political oratory (public speaking). Quoting from the Bible, Lincoln avowed, " 'A house divided against itself cannot stand.' I believe this government cannot endure permanently half *slave* and half *free*. I do not expect the Union to be *dissolved*—I do not expect the house to *fall*—but I *do* expect it will cease to be divided. It will become *all* one thing, or *all* the other."

Lincoln, undoubtedly hoping to bask in some of his better-known rival's limelight, challenged Douglas to a series of joint debates throughout Illinois. Douglas reluctantly agreed. He worried that Lincoln was "the strong man of his party—full of wit, facts, dates—and the best stump speaker . . . in the West." The debaters presented a startling contrast: tall, thin Abe Lincoln, carelessly dressed in a rumpled, well-worn suit, his unruly dark hair springing out in all directions; and short, stocky Stephen Douglas, elegantly attired in a ruffled shirt, impeccably tailored frock coat, and stylish white hat. Despite his plain appearance, Lincoln's moral passion and keen logic—not to mention his knack for telling funny stories—won over many of his listeners.

Lincoln repeatedly characterized slavery as a great moral evil during the debates, but Douglas refused to judge the institution as either right or wrong. Sharply aware of the widespread prejudice against blacks in

Lincoln and Douglas engaged in seven debates while they campaigned for the Illinois State Senate seat in 1858. Douglas's fine clothing and elegant manner made him appear to be the superior man, but it was Lincoln's moral conviction and talent for public speaking that won over the audiences. Although Lincoln did not win that election, he earned the nationwide recognition he would build on for the 1860 presidential election.

Illinois, Douglas frequently accused Lincoln of being an undercover abolitionist who would let freed slaves take white men's jobs and marry their daughters. Although ahead of most Americans of his time in his racial views, in 1858, Lincoln still shared the popular belief that the races were unequal. In response to Douglas's persistent attacks, an exasperated Lincoln finally declared that he was not in favor of political equality for blacks—of "making voters . . . of negroes, nor of qualifying them to hold office." Nonetheless, he maintained, *all* human beings were entitled to the "unalienable natural rights enumerated in the Declaration of Independence, the right to life, liberty, and the pursuit of happiness." A black man unquestionably had every bit as much right to enjoy the fruits of his labor as a white man did, Lincoln emphasized.

In the end, because of an outdated system for apportioning seats in the Illinois legislature, Douglas kept his Senate seat, even though Republican candidates actually received more votes than Democratic ones. (It should be remembered that senators were elected by state legislators, not by direct popular vote.) Nonetheless, the seven Lincoln–Douglas debates, which were covered by major national newspapers, showcased Lincoln's political talents and brought him to the attention of Americans far beyond Illinois's borders. Consequently, Lincoln's Republican associates began encouraging him to seek the presidential nomination for the upcoming election in 1860.

THE ELECTION OF 1860

At the urging of his supporters, Lincoln started accepting requests to speak outside Illinois. On February 27, 1860, he delivered a highly publicized address at Cooper Union in New York City. Meant to introduce him and his views on slavery to eastern Republicans, the talk was a complete success. As one listener recalled, "When Lincoln rose to speak, I was greatly disappointed. He was . . . so angular and awkward." As Lincoln warmed to his subject, the audience member found himself completely won over by the gawky man's sincerity and passion: "[H]is face lighted up as with an inward fire; the whole man was transfigured. I forgot his clothes, his personal appearance, and his individual peculiarities. Presently, forgetting myself, I was on my feet like the rest . . . cheering this wonderful man."

"Neither let us be slandered from our duty by false accusations against us, nor frightened from it by menaces of destruction to the Government nor of dungeons to ourselves. Let us have faith that right makes might, and in that faith, let us, to the end, dare to do our duty as we understand it."

— With these words, Lincoln closed his address at the Cooper Union. In the speech, he urged Republicans to stand up for their principles despite Southern accusations that their fight to keep slavery out of the territories was unconstitutional and motivated by purely "sectional" interests

Three months later, Republicans met in Chicago to choose their presidential candidate. Although Senator William Seward of New York led on the first ballot, by the third ballot, Lincoln—widely considered more moderate on slavery and therefore the safer candidate— had captured the nomination. His running mate was Hannibal Hamlin of Maine.

Meanwhile, the Democrats, bitterly split between Northern and Southern wings, could not agree on a presidential candidate. The Southerners ultimately nominated

John C. Breckinridge of Kentucky and the Northerners nominated Stephen Douglas. Once trusted by slaveholders, Douglas had gravely offended them when he stated in one of his debates with Lincoln that slavery, which Southerners liked to think of as a humane institution, could not exist "a day or an hour anywhere" without the rigorous backing of the local police. The field became even more crowded when John Bell of Tennessee entered the race representing the Constitutional Union party, formed to preserve the Union in the face of the secessionist threats increasingly being made by the most militant Southerners or "fire-eaters."

Hoping to appeal to the small farmers and laborers who made up most of the Northern voting public, Lincoln's political handlers presented him as a man of the people, christening him the "Illinois Rail-Splitter" and "Honest Abe." They printed handbills and organized big parades and rallies to promote their man, but Lincoln himself stayed at home in Springfield in keeping with the long-standing custom that presidential candidates did not campaign for themselves. Indeed, there would have been little reason for Lincoln to hit the campaign trial. With the Democratic Party split, his election was practically assured.

In November 1860, although he polled just 39 percent of the popular vote, Lincoln won a decisive majority in the electoral college, taking every Northern state but New Jersey. In the lower South, however, he did not receive a single vote. The election results dramatically underlined the rift between North and South, which had been

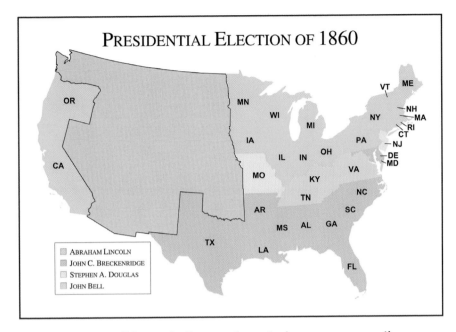

PRESIDENTIAL ELECTION OF 1860

ABRAHAM LINCOLN
JOHN C. BRECKENRIDGE
STEPHEN A. DOUGLAS
JOHN BELL

Although Lincoln did not win the popular vote, he won every northern state except for New Jersey in the electoral college, as this map of the 1860 presidential election shows. The split votes between the Democrats for John C. Breckenridge and Stephen A. Douglas greatly contributed to Lincoln's win.

growing even wider over the past several years after South Carolinian Preston Brooks physically assaulted Charles Sumner, an antislavery Northerner, on the Senate floor; the controversial Dred Scott decision, in which Chief Justice Roger Taney declared, among other things, that Congress could not forbid slavery in the territories; the ongoing violence between pro- and antislavery settlers and their supporters in "Bleeding Kansas"; and finally, in 1859, abolitionist John Brown's failed attempt to start a slave revolt by raiding a government arsenal (military storehouse) at Harpers Ferry, Virginia.

Abraham Lincoln appears in these prints as a presidential candidate in 1860 (left) and as president in 1861 (right). During the presidential campaign, 11-year-old Grace Bedell of New York wrote to Lincoln and advised him to grow a beard. "You would look a good deal better" and "since all the ladies like whiskers," she explained, wives would convince "their husbands to vote for you." An amused Lincoln decided to take Grace's advice.

Although Lincoln carefully distanced himself from the abolitionists, declaring repeatedly that he would not interfere with slavery in the states where it was already established, Southern politicians and newspaper editors twisted Lincoln's antislavery views during the campaign, making them sound far more radical than they were. Also, although three-quarters of Southern families did not own a single slave, militant slaveholders managed to convince the region's non-slaveholding majority that antislavery Northerners like Lincoln were bent on trampling their rights as well. Consequently, between Lincoln's election and February 1, 1861, seven Southern states pulled out of the Union. As the president-elect bade farewell to his friends and neighbors in Springfield and boarded a train for Washington, D.C. on February 11, seven more slave states wavered between the Union and the Confederacy. Never before had a president assumed office under such perilous circumstances. Before him, Lincoln believed, lay a task even "greater than that which rested upon [President] Washington."

"I now leave, not knowing when, or whether ever, I may return, with a task before me greater than that which rested upon Washington. Without the assistance of the Divine Being, who ever attended him, I cannot succeed. With that assistance I cannot fail. Trusting in Him . . . let us confidently hope that all will yet be well."

— From Lincoln's Farewell Address at Springfield, Illinois, February 11, 1861, delivered right before the president-elect boarded the train that would carry him to his inauguration in Washington, D.C.

4

"To Save
the Union":
1861–1863

WHEN LINCOLN ARRIVED in Washington, D.C., on February 23, 1861, seven states—South Carolina, Mississippi, Florida, Alabama, Georgia, Louisiana, and Texas—had already formed their own government, the Confederate States of America, with Jefferson Davis as president. Four other states of the upper South—Virginia, North Carolina, Tennessee, and Arkansas— appeared on the verge of seceding, and disunion sentiment was strong in three border slave states—Kentucky, Missouri, and Maryland.

Although appalled by secession, President Buchanan hesitated to act against the Confederacy during the lame-duck period

In this artist's rendering from *Frank Leslie's Illustrated Newspaper,*
Jefferson Davis, who was elected president of the Confederate
States of America, addresses the people of Montgomery, Alabama on
February 16, 1861. Seven southern states formed the Confederacy
when Lincoln, an antislavery candidate, won the U.S. presidency.

(the time between when a new president is elected and
when he takes office) lasting until Lincoln's inauguration in March. Meanwhile, Congress debated several
different compromise plans. The most important, the

Crittendon Compromise, sought to end the crisis by splitting the territories between free and slave. The president-elect, however, made it clear that he would never support a proposal involving the extension of slavery, and the scheme quickly died.

THE CIVIL WAR BEGINS

During the final weeks of Buchanan's presidency, the Confederates took control of most federal forts in the lower South. In his inaugural speech, Lincoln warned the secessionists that he would not allow any more military bases to be seized, declaring, "The power confided to me, will be used to hold, occupy, and possess the property, and places belonging to the government." A showdown was inevitable. It came barely a month after inauguration day, when Lincoln announced he was shipping supplies to Fort Sumter off the South Carolina coast, suggesting that he planned to hold the island base indefinitely. The Confederates responded on April 12 by bombarding Fort Sumter. After two days of heavy shelling, the approximately 70 U.S. troops stationed at the fort surrendered and were permitted to sail back north. The Civil War had begun.

Lincoln moved quickly in the wake of the attack on Fort Sumter. With a regular army of just 16,000, the federal government was woefully unprepared for war. Therefore, on April 15, Lincoln ordered the states to provide 75,000 volunteers to fight for the restoration of the Union. Virginia, North Carolina, Tennessee, and Arkansas reacted by promptly joining the Confederacy. In Kentucky,

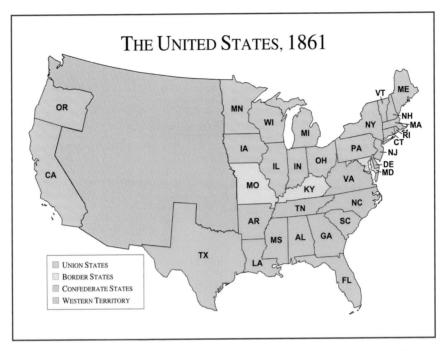

The rift between the north and south sharpened dramatically when the strongly antislavery Lincoln was elected president, as this map of the United States in 1861 illustrates. Eleven southern states ultimately seceded, with the border states of Missouri, Kentucky, and Maryland just barely remaining in the Union.

Maryland, and Missouri, Unionist loyalties prevailed over secessionist sentiment in the spring of 1861, but did so by an alarmingly narrow margin. Indeed, secessionist sympathies were so powerful in Maryland that for a period of time, Washington, D.C. was cut off from all communication with the North after pro-Confederate mobs in Baltimore ripped down telegraph wires and destroyed railroad bridges north of the city. Lincoln took the drastic measure of suspending the writ of habeas corpus (which prohibits imprisonment without trial) for all people living between

Philadelphia and Washington, D.C., to help reestablish order and secure Maryland's loyalty in the future.

North of the border states, the response to Lincoln's call to arms was enthusiastic: Confident the war would be quickly won, volunteers flooded into the capital. After increasing the size of the regular army and navy by executive order, Lincoln was well on his way to building a formidable armed force. Now the Union needed a military strategy, which General in Chief Scott soon provided. Scott's relatively bloodless "anaconda" plan, named for a constrictor snake, would slowly strangle the Confederacy by taking control of the Mississippi River and tightening the naval blockade of Southern seaports that Lincoln began after the Fort Sumter attack. Lincoln, however, had serious doubts about the plan. Worried that Scott's scheme would take too long, he believed that the Union must grab the offensive and invade the South. In July, Lincoln ordered General Irvin McDowell to attack the large Confederate army at Manassas, Virginia, about 25 miles south of Washington, D.C., and take the best direct route to the Confederate capital at Richmond.

On July 21, 1861, Confederate and Union forces fought along Bull Run stream near Manassas in the first major battle of the Civil War. The inexperienced Union troops performed well at first, but when their line broke, they fled back north in confusion. In the wake of this humiliating event, Lincoln ordered General George B. McClellan, a skilled organizer and administrator, to take charge of the main Union army, the Army of the Potomac. Lincoln also composed a memorandum on military policy that called for tightening the naval blockade on the South and recruiting and training long-term volunteers. When the forces were ready, a three-pronged offensive down the Mississippi River, in Tennessee, and in Virginia would be launched to overwhelm the Confederates with larger forces on several fronts at the same time.

THE NEW PRESIDENT CONFRONTS OTHER CHALLENGES

Although Lincoln considered overseeing the Union war effort his chief responsibility, he could not give all his time to military issues. Before the civil service was created to fill federal posts, the president was expected to personally name every government officeholder. Consequently, much of Lincoln's time was taken up with meeting the armies of office-seekers who began descending on the White House on the first day of his administration. Lincoln also devoted many hours to meeting the hundreds of others who lined up to see him, including not only congressmen and foreign dignitaries but also ordinary citizens looking for favors or just hoping to shake the president's hand. To his staff's dismay, Lincoln was determined to meet every one of them. "They do not want much, and they get very little," he declared. "I know how I would feel in their place." Lincoln also believed that his visits with private citizens helped him gauge public opinion on the war and other critical issues. Although much of the Northern press was harshly critical of the "Illinois Rail-splitter," blasting

The First Lady loved to wear expensive clothing and jewelry and had a fondness for costly furnishings. Lincoln was furious when Mary suggested that he ask Congress for additional funds to cover her exorbitant bills to redecorate the White House, saying he would pay the bills "out of my own pocket first" rather than make Congress pay for "flub dubs—for this damn old house, when the soldiers cannot have blankets!"

the new president as ignorant and unqualified, Lincoln's willingness to make himself available to the public won him the affection of many ordinary Northerners, who christened him "Father Abraham."

Although Lincoln's relations with the northern masses were generally positive during the early months of his administration, his relations with his cabinet were less satisfactory. Hoping to unite his party, Lincoln assigned cabinet positions to radical antislavery Republicans as well as those with moderate views on slavery, to former Democrats as well as former Whigs. Thus he gave the secretary of state post to his chief rival for the Republican presidential nomination in 1860, one-time Whig William Seward, and made the ambitious Salmon P. Chase, another rival for the nomination and an ex-Democrat, secretary of the treasury.

Lincoln gave the diverse and fiercely opinioned men who served in his cabinet almost free reign in running their departments, but from the start, he refused to let them infringe on his own authority. When Seward proposed that he assume the day-to-day running of the executive branch because Lincoln lacked adminis-trative experience, Lincoln tactfully but firmly declined the secretary of state's offer. Also, when it became clear that his haughty secretary of war, Simon Cameron, was both inefficient and corrupt, Lincoln forced him to resign and replaced him with Edwin M. Stanton, who was every bit as strong-willed as Cameron but far more competent and honest.

A TIME OF HOPE AND OF SORROW

Meanwhile, on the military front, Lincoln began to have doubts about the man he had chosen to lead the federal forces. McClellan had done such a fine job training the 250,000 soldiers of the Army of the Potomac that in November, Lincoln had made him commander of all the Union armies. As 1861 turned into 1862, however, McClellan had still made no move to use the troops he had organized and drilled. Finally, after months of hedging, McClellan informed Lincoln that he planned to transport his troops to the coast of Virginia and advance on Richmond from the east. Lincoln thought a frontal assault on the large Confederate army at Manassas would make more sense. Nonetheless, acknowledging McClellan's greater military expertise, Lincoln approved the general's plan.

In early 1862, despite his worries about McClellan's handling of the war in the east, Lincoln had good reason to feel hopeful about the military situation in the western theater (west of the Appalachian Mountains). On February 6 and February 17, a relatively unknown Union general named Ulysses S. Grant captured two strategically vital forts—Henry and Donelson—on the Tennessee and Cumberland rivers, thereby opening a path into Tennessee, Alabama, and Mississippi for the northern forces.

Lincoln's joy over the Union victories in Tennessee was to be short-lived. On February 20, the president suffered a devastating loss when his 11-year-old son, Willie, died of typhoid. Years earlier, he and Mary had lost another young son, Eddie, to illness, and the death of a second—and by

This famous 1864 portrait of Lincoln with his youngest son, Tad, appears to show the president reading a book to his child. In reality, father and son were looking at a photograph album together. Tad died from tuberculosis in 1871 when he was just 18 years old. Lincoln's eldest child, Robert, was the only among his four children to live into adulthood.

many accounts, favorite—child was a crushing blow to both parents. Mary, who had long suffered from emotional instability, was pushed to the brink of complete mental breakdown by this new family tragedy. Although prone to periodic bouts of depression himself, Lincoln could not afford to surrender to his grief when he had the responsibilities of a wartime presidency resting on his shoulders. He threw himself into his work with grim determination, devoting whatever time he had left at the end of the day to his youngest son, Tad, who was recovering from the same illness that had claimed Willie's life. (The Lincolns' other surviving child, Robert, was away in Massachusetts attending Harvard College during most of Lincoln's presidency.)

McCLELLAN'S POOR LEADERSHIP

Union forces scored an important victory in April 1862, when they captured New Orleans, the Confederacy's chief port but the spring and summer of 1862 generally brought a worrisome downturn in the North's military fortunes. At the Battle of Shiloh in Tennessee, Grant managed to defeat his Confederate attackers, but at a terrible cost—more than 10,000 Union soldiers were killed or wounded and another 3,000 went missing, leaving the western army seriously depleted.

In the East, McClellan's army arrived on the Virginia coast in early April and began inching its way toward Richmond. To Lincoln's dismay, the ever-cautious general kept putting off his planned assault on the Confederate capital. "You must act," the president finally wrote to McClellan in exasperation. While McClellan procrastinated, the Confederates sent additional troops to the Richmond area and built intricate defenses around their capital. When McClellan finally began his push toward Richmond in earnest on June 25, the Army of the Potomac found itself caught in seven days of intense fighting against a formidable enemy. By the end of these "Seven Days' Battles," the federal forces had been turned back.

Because of McClellan's floundering, Lincoln appointed

John Pope to be the new commander for the army in northern Virginia and scholarly Henry "Old Brains" Halleck to be the new general in chief for all the Union armies. Although Pope was certainly more aggressive than McClellan, his crushing defeat at the Second Battle of Bull Run in August 1862 convinced Lincoln to give McClellan one more chance with the Army of the Potomac. With his multi-front plan in danger of collapsing altogether, however, Lincoln decided he must take a bigger role in steering Northern strategy. From late summer 1862 until March 1864, when he finally made Ulysses S. Grant commander of the Union armies, Lincoln practically directed Union military strategy himself. "Old Brains" Halleck completely lost his nerve after the humiliating defeat at the Second Battle of Bull Run, and from then on, according to Lincoln, acted more like a "first-rate clerk" than the nation's chief strategic planner.

Shortly after the Second Battle of Bull Run, the Confederates launched a bold offensive against the North with Robert E. Lee and the Army of Northern Virginia pushing across the Potomac River into Maryland. On September 17, larger Union forces under McClellan intercepted the Confederates at Sharpsburg near Antietam Creek. The battle was the single bloodiest day of the entire war, leaving more than 23,000 men killed or wounded. Although McClellan forced Lee's retreat, he failed to pursue him energetically, thus losing an extraordinary opportunity to destroy Lee's big army. Lincoln's patience with McClellan's "overcautiousness" finally came to an end, and the president stripped McClellan of his command over the main Union army once and for all in November 1862, replacing him with Ambrose Burnside. Five days after the Battle of Antietam, Lincoln took another even more significant step in his role as commander in chief when he issued what would come to be known as the Preliminary Emancipation Proclamation.

MOVING TOWARD EMANCIPATION

Lincoln had been under pressure to outlaw slavery in the states as well as the territories since the beginning of his presidency. Some of this pressure originated outside the country: All of Europe was appalled by the continuation of slavery in the United States. Lincoln had reason to be particularly concerned about the opinion of England, the chief European power. Antislavery sentiment ran high in England, but because its textile mills used massive quantities of Southern cotton, Lincoln still worried that British leaders might support the Confederacy. In the Trent Affair in 1861, Lincoln even intervened in foreign affairs—an area he usually left to Secretary of State Seward—in order to appease the British. The Trent Affair began when a Union naval officer forcibly removed two Confederate envoys from a British ship. To placate the offended British government, Lincoln personally ordered the Confederates' release. Nonetheless, though Lincoln realized that taking decisive action against slavery could only improve the Union's standing in England and throughout Europe, he was determined to approach emancipation cautiously.

The new president had to resist even more pressure

from within the United States to act quickly against slavery. Most of it came from Congress, specifically from the radical antislavery wing of Lincoln's own party (generally known as the Radicals). On issues concerning the economy, Lincoln stuck firmly to the Whig tradition that Congress, not the president, should shape legislation, and promptly signed congressional bills to create a national banking system and currency and to provide assistance to poor Easterners seeking to settle in the West with the Homestead Act. On anything concerning war policy, however, he stubbornly resisted Congress's efforts to tell him what to do. Viewing the issue of slavery as closely linked to his war policy, Lincoln also refused to let Congress dictate to him regarding emancipation.

Lincoln's determination to retain control over when—if at all—the slaves would be freed was tied to his concerns regarding Kentucky, Missouri, and Maryland, where pro-Confederate sentiment remained strong. He worried that any action by the federal government against slavery might drive these wavering border slave states right out of the Union. If that happened, he believed, the Union cause was as good as dead.

In March 1862, the president took some tentative steps toward emancipation by asking the states to consider a plan for gradual emancipation in which slave-owners would receive compensation from the government for their slaves and freed slaves would be encouraged to settle in Central America or Africa. (Lincoln's colonization scheme was nothing new—over the years, many leaders, including Thomas Jefferson, Andrew Jackson, and Henry Clay, had suggested settling freed slaves outside the United States.) Yet as conservative and mild as Lincoln's plan was, not a single border state representative would back it, and leading black Americans such as abolitionist Frederick Douglass were deeply offended by the proposal's emphasis on sending freedmen abroad.

A few months later, impatient congressional Radicals sought to take emancipation into their own hands by passing legislation to confiscate and free the slaves of anyone who supported the Confederacy. Still deeply worried about the border states, Lincoln hesitated to enforce the

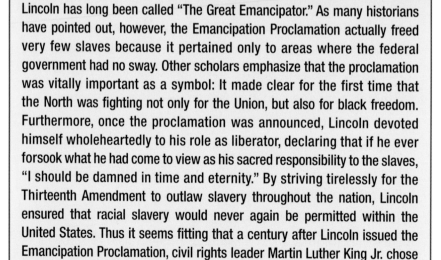

PRESIDENT LINCOLN'S LEGACY

Freeing the Slaves

Lincoln has long been called "The Great Emancipator." As many historians have pointed out, however, the Emancipation Proclamation actually freed very few slaves because it pertained only to areas where the federal government had no sway. Other scholars emphasize that the proclamation was vitally important as a symbol: It made clear for the first time that the North was fighting not only for the Union, but also for black freedom. Furthermore, once the proclamation was announced, Lincoln devoted himself wholeheartedly to his role as liberator, declaring that if he ever forsook what he had come to view as his sacred responsibility to the slaves, "I should be damned in time and eternity." By striving tirelessly for the Thirteenth Amendment to outlaw slavery throughout the nation, Lincoln ensured that racial slavery would never again be permitted within the United States. Thus it seems fitting that a century after Lincoln issued the Emancipation Proclamation, civil rights leader Martin Luther King Jr. chose to deliver his historic "I Have a Dream" speech in front of the Lincoln Memorial in Washington, D.C.

act. This infuriated antislavery editor Horace Greeley, who publicly criticized the president for dragging his feet on emancipation in Greeley's newspaper *The New York Tribune.* In his reply to Greeley, Lincoln emphasized that although he wished all people could be free, he could not allow his public policy to be determined by his private feelings. Whatever he decided to do—or not do—regarding emancipation would be done to "save the Union," because he firmly believed that restoring the Union was his most important duty as president. What Lincoln

"As to the policy I 'seem to be pursuing' as you say, I have not meant to leave any one in doubt.

I would save the Union. . . . If I could save the Union without freeing any slave I would do it, and if I could save it by freeing all the slaves I would do it; and if I could save it by freeing some and leaving others alone I would also do that. . . .

I have here stated my purpose according to my view of official duty; and I intend no modification of my oft-expressed personal wish that all men every where could be free."

— From Lincoln's letter of August 22, 1862 to Horace Greeley in response to Greeley's call for Lincoln to place freeing the slaves at the center of his war policy

chose not reveal to Greeley was that by the time his letter was written in August, he had already committed himself to pushing ahead with emancipation.

LINCOLN ISSUES HIS EMANCIPATION PROCLAMATIONS

By the summer of 1862, Lincoln had concluded that his gradual and voluntary emancipation plan of the previous spring was going nowhere. On July 22, therefore, Lincoln presented a draft for an emancipation proclamation to his cabinet. Secretary Seward persuaded Lincoln to wait for a military victory before issuing the decree; otherwise, he warned, it might appear as an act of desperation in the wake of a string of Union defeats. Victory finally came at Antietam and five days later, on September 22, Lincoln introduced his new emancipation plan to the nation.

Lincoln's Preliminary Emancipation Proclamation announced that in 100 days he would free the slaves within any state still in rebellion against the U.S. government. On January 1, 1863, as promised, Lincoln issued his final Emancipation Proclamation, signing it in the presence of his entire cabinet. One important change had been made in the document since September: The final proclamation stipulated that for the first time, former slaves would be permitted to join the federal army. By the end of the war, nearly 180,000 black Americans were serving in the Union forces.

Lincoln had long acknowledged that the Constitution did not permit the federal government to interfere with slavery in the states. In the Emancipation Proclamation, he got around this difficulty by basing his authority to free the slaves on his war powers as commander in chief, which included the right to seize a military opponent's "property." Because the proclamation was grounded on the president's war powers, it was only valid in those areas of the country actually controlled by the Confederates, and not in slave states still within the Union (in other words, the worrisome border states) or in those parts of the Confederacy occupied by Union troops. Consequently, when it was issued on January 1, the proclamation actually liberated few slaves. Nonetheless, it was immensely important as a symbol: It showed that the federal government was no longer only fighting for reunion; it was also fighting against slavery.

The Emancipation Proclamation fell far short of the expectations of the Radicals and of some Europeans, but because it redefined the war as a struggle for freedom, most antislavery Americans lauded the document. On the other hand, because it left slavery alone in the loyal border states, the proclamation did not alienate the citizens of those strategically critical areas at a time when the final outcome of the war was still in doubt. Most historians today agree that the Emancipation Proclamation was a document of remarkable political insight, ingeniously suited to the particular circumstances and challenges of the time at which it was written.

> *"Fellow-citizens, we cannot escape history. We of this Congress and this administration, will be remembered in spite of ourselves. . . . The fiery trial through which we pass, will light us down, in honor or dishonor, to the latest generation. . . . We know how to save the Union. . . . In giving freedom to the slave, we assure freedom to the free—honorable alike in what we give, and what we preserve. We shall nobly save, or meanly lose, the last best, hope of earth. . . ."*
>
> — These eloquent words are from Lincoln's December 1862 message to Congress, delivered a little more than two months after his Preliminary Emancipation Proclamation

5

"THE ALMIGHTY HAS HIS OWN PURPOSES": 1863–1865

WITHIN WEEKS OF issuing the Emancipation Proclamation, Lincoln appointed yet another general, Joseph Hooker, to lead the Army of the Potomac after Burnside led a series of ill-planned and horribly deadly assaults on Confederate positions at Fredericksburg, Virginia. Lincoln was quickly disappointed with Hooker: Under his command, the Army of the Potomac fell to a much smaller Confederate army at the Battle of Chancellorsville in May 1863. By June, Lincoln's ongoing search for a general capable of bringing a Union victory had led him to replace Hooker with George Meade of Pennsylvania. Aware that Lee was planning a new offensive that would take him into Meade's home state, Lincoln

Encamped at Cumberland Landing, Virginia, in 1862, the Union Army of the Potomac went on to fight in the Battle of Gettysburg in Pennsylvania under the leadership of George Meade. Union general Ulysses S. Grant added to the Gettysburg victory a day later when he captured Vicksburg, Mississippi.

figured the general would "fight well on his own dunghill."

As it turned out, Lincoln was right. At the Battle of Gettsyburg in southern Pennsylvania, Meade turned back Lee's invasion in a fierce three-day contest that left 50,000 men dead or wounded. Despite the general's victory at Gettysburg, Lincoln was frustrated by Meade's failure to pursue and destroy Lee's forces following the battle—an omission similar to McClellan having allowed Lee and his army to escape after the Battle of Antietam.

The Gettysburg Address

Lincoln's Gettysburg Address, presented at the November 19, 1863 dedication ceremonies for a national cemetery on the Gettsyburg battlefield, is probably the most famous speech ever delivered by an American president, and according to many scholars, by far, the most eloquent:

Four score and seven years ago our fathers brought forth on this continent, a new nation, conceived in Liberty, and dedicated to the proposition that all men are created equal.

Now we are engaged in a great civil war, testing whether that nation, or any nation so conceived and so dedicated, can long endure. We are met on a great battlefield of that war. We have come to dedicate a portion of that field, as a final resting place for those who here gave their lives that that nation might live. It is altogether fitting and proper that we should do this.

But, in a larger sense, we cannot dedicate—we cannot consecrate—we cannot hallow—this ground. The brave men, living and dead, who struggled here, have consecrated it, far above our poor power to add or detract. The world will little note, nor long remember what we say here, but it can never forget what they did here. It is for us the living, rather, to be dedicated here to the unfinished work which they who fought here have thus far so nobly advanced. It is rather for us to be here dedicated to the great task remaining before us—that from these honored dead we take increased devotion to that cause for which they gave the last full measure of devotion—that we here highly resolve that these dead shall not have died in vain—that this nation, under God, shall have a new birth of freedom—and that government of the people, by the people, for the people, shall not perish from the earth.

On July 4, 1863, one day after the Union win at Gettsyburg, Grant scored another important victory for the North when he captured Vicksburg, Mississippi, and gave federal forces control of the entire Mississippi River. Lincoln was so impressed by Grant's performance at Vicksburg that in early 1864, he appointed him general in chief of the Union forces, keeping Meade as commander of the Army of the Potomac. Lincoln had found in Ulysses S. Grant a commander in whom he had complete confidence.

LINCOLN CONFRONTS ANTIWAR SENTIMENT

Throughout the Civil War, antiwar sentiment was generally stronger in the South than the North, a phenomenon some historians credit to Lincoln's tireless efforts to reach out to the common people. In his speeches and correspondence, Lincoln let the American people know that he understood and shared their suffering. The most famous letter of condolence he wrote during the war was to Lydia Bixby, who lost five sons in the fighting. In his moving letter, which was widely reprinted in Northern newspapers, Lincoln wrote:

> I feel how weak and fruitless must be any words of mine which should attempt to beguile you from the grief of a loss so overwhelming. . . . I pray that our Heavenly Father may assuage [ease] the anguish of your bereavement [grief], and leave you only the cherished memory of the loved and lost, and the solemn pride that must be yours, to have laid so costly a sacrifice upon the altar of Freedom.

Although Lincoln's compassionate words helped maintain broad popular support for the war, antiwar feeling still persisted in some factions in the North, as the New York City Draft Riots of July 1863 demonstrate. As was also true of Southern draft regulations, Union draft laws discriminated against the poor because wealthy men could pay a fee to get out of the draft or hire substitutes to fight for them in the war. The New York City riots were not the only protest against unjust draft rules in the North, but they were by far the most violent. After three days of arson and murder — mainly of escaped slaves by poor whites who feared that freedmen would steal their jobs — federal soldiers finally put down the disturbance.

Despite the mob violence in New York, most antiwar activity in the North was confined to the realm of politics and more specifically to the Democratic Party. Although some party members were "War Democrats," who believed the crisis between North and South could be solved only by military means, many others were "Peace Democrats" — or Copperheads, as they were also known — who wanted an immediate cease-fire and a negotiated settlement between North and South. Copperheads appealed not only to the war weariness of their Northern supporters but also to racial prejudices. Most strongly opposed the Emancipation Proclamation, saying that Lincoln had no right to ask white men to fight a "war for the Negro."

Peace Democrats also criticized Lincoln for what

they considered tyrannical abuse of his executive powers. Lincoln repeatedly suspended the writ of habeas corpus in the North during the course of the war and even allowed his generals to briefly suspend several stridently antiwar newspapers. Scholars have debated whether Lincoln's actions were appropriate given the grave dangers of the time. While the Civil War raged, Lincoln assumed greater executive authority than any president before him, not only ordering imprisonment without trial for civilians suspected of disloyalty, but also establishing a blockade and increasing the size of the regular armed forces while Congress was not in session. Both of those actions normally required Congress's authorization.

THE ELECTION OF 1864

Despite the claims of his opponents, perhaps the strongest evidence that Lincoln was not a "tyrant" was that he did not use the war as an excuse to cancel or postpone the presidential election of 1864, although throughout the previous summer he believed he would lose. There was probably greater discontent regarding the war among Northerners during the summer of 1864 than at any time before. The fighting had been dragging on for three full years, and Grant's new offensive in Virginia was proving extremely costly: Between May and June, 60,000 Union soldiers were wounded or killed. Hoping to benefit from Northern war weariness, the Democrats nominated General George B. McClellan

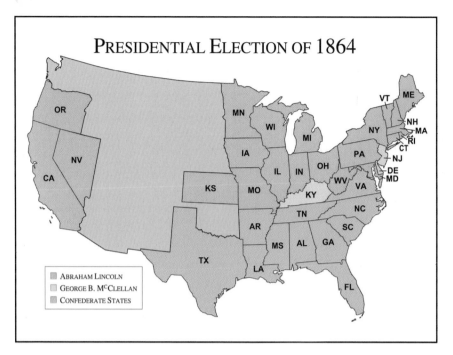

PRESIDENTIAL ELECTION OF 1864

ABRAHAM LINCOLN
GEORGE B. MⁱCCLELLAN
CONFEDERATE STATES

Although Lincoln feared he would lose his bid for reelection in 1864, a string of Union victories prior to the election brought hope to the north and greater faith in their president. Lincoln won all of the northern and border states except for Delaware, Kentucky, and New Jersey, which were taken by George B. McClellan.

for president and adopted a platform calling for a truce and peace conference.

At the Republican National Convention in May, although many Radicals would have preferred to replace him with one of their own, Lincoln had enough support to win the nomination on the first ballot. Andrew Johnson, a pro-Union War Democrat from Tennessee, was nominated as vice president, replacing Hannibal Hamlin. During the campaign, the Republicans called themselves the "Union Party" to emphasize their strong commitment to restoring the Union and that their candidates represented an alliance of North and South, Republican and Democrat.

Lincoln adamantly insisted that the Union platform include a plank calling for an amendment outlawing racial slavery throughout the United States. Lincoln may have been slow to embrace emancipation in the first place, but once he issued his proclamation, he committed himself completely to ensuring the future freedom of the slaves. Fearing that the Supreme Court would strike down the Emancipation Proclamation, Lincoln believed that a constitutional amendment was the only way to guarantee that slavery would not be reestablished in the nation once the war was over. "Sink or swim, live or die, survive or perish," he pledged, "I give my heart and hand to this measure."

During the months following the Republican convention, as Union casualties continued to mount and peace appeared as far away as ever, Lincoln had little faith that he could prevail at the polls. Like many Americans, he was starting to wonder if the rebels would ever give up and if the bloodshed would ever end. "I cannot bear it," a gaunt and exhausted Lincoln confessed to a friend, this "suffering, this loss of life . . ." As the summer drew to a close, however, Admiral David Farragut captured the vital Confederate port of Mobile, Alabama, and Grant's subordinate, General William Tecumseh Sherman, conquered Atlanta. Lincoln and the entire North began to hope again. The November election reflected the improving military situation: When the votes were counted, Lincoln had carried all the Northern and border states except New Jersey, Delaware, and Kentucky.

Immediately after his reelection, Lincoln began pressing Congress to approve an amendment abolishing racial slavery forever. By late January 1865, largely because of his tireless efforts, Congress had passed the Thirteenth Amendment and on February 1, a jubilant Lincoln submitted it to the states for ratification. "The great job is ended," he declared. "I . . . congratulate . . . myself, the country, and the whole world upon this great moral victory."

LINCOLN'S SECOND INAUGURATION

It had been rainy and overcast all day when, at 1:00 P.M. on March 4, Lincoln rose from his seat on the platform in front of the Capitol to deliver his Second Inaugural Address. As he began to speak, the sun broke through the heavy clouds so abruptly that "it made my heart jump," Lincoln later said. The 30,000 spectators crowded into the plaza below listened quietly as the president, whose haggard face mirrored the toll four years of war had taken on him, told them what they knew only too well: Neither Northerners nor Southerners had "expected for the war, the magnitude, or the duration, which it has already attained." The president went on to offer an explanation for the devastating length and intensity of the war that probably surprised just about everyone in his audience.

In March 1865, it was evident that the war—as well as the Confederacy—was all but finished: Sherman had taken Savannah, Georgia, and was marching north

In the speech on the occasion of his second inauguration, Lincoln strove to unite the country by refusing to place blame for the Civil War on the South alone. Instead, he insisted that the entire United States shared the guilt. His famous speech ended with a request for his countrymen to treat each other "with malice toward none; with charity for all."

through the Carolinas; and Grant had severed all supply routes to Lee's army at Petersburg, just south of Richmond, Virginia. Instead of congratulating his listeners and himself on the hard-earned victory they would shortly be enjoying, however, Lincoln emphasized that both North and South must take responsibility for the war and the suffering it had caused for four long years.

The entire conflict, Lincoln asserted, could only be

understood within a religious context. If Lincoln's audience expected him to assure them that God was and had always been on their side, as demonstrated by the imminent Union victory, they were sorely disappointed. What Lincoln said instead was that God's understanding of the war and their interpretation of it were not necessarily the same. "The Almighty has His own purposes" in allowing the "mighty scourge" of civil war to devastate the nation, he declared. Could it be, Lincoln wondered, that God meant the war as a punishment on all white Americans—Northern and Southern alike—for allowing the terrible sin of racial slavery in their land for nearly two centuries before finally moving to strike it down?

If both sides shared the guilt for the coming of the war, as Lincoln was suggesting, then it was clearly unjust for the North to seek revenge against the defeated South. Thus, on the verge of victory, Lincoln chose to close his extraordinary inaugural address with a plea for a compassionate and generous peace: "With malice toward none; with charity for all; . . . let us strive . . . to bind up the nation's wounds . . . to do all which may achieve and cherish a just, and a lasting peace. . . ."

LINCOLN AND RECONSTRUCTION

Since the earliest days of the war, Lincoln had given a great deal of thought to Reconstruction, the program by which the Confederate states would be restored to the Union. From the start, he wanted a plan that would embody the sentiments he expressed in the final paragraph of his Second Inaugural Address: "with malice toward none; with charity for all." In December 1863, with Tennessee, Arkansas, and Louisiana largely occupied by Union armies, Lincoln had put forth his "ten percent plan," which would grant amnesty to most rebels who took an oath of loyalty to the United States and federal recognition of new state governments after just ten percent of a state's voting population took the oath. When Arkansas set up a state government under the ten percent plan, however, Congress denied the new administration's request to have its senators and representatives seated. Instead, blasting Lincoln's plan as too lenient, the Radicals created their own far harsher Reconstruction plan, the Wade–Davis Bill, in July 1864. This bill would readmit a state only after a majority of white adult males had taken the loyalty oath. To the Radicals' fury, Lincoln, asserting that he was unprepared "to be inflexibly committed to any single plan of restoration," pocket vetoed the bill. (By presenting the Wade-Davis Bill to Lincoln just days before adjourning, Congress inadvertently allowed him to use his presidential pocket veto to defeat it by holding—or pocketing—the unsigned bill until after adjournment.)

On April 11, 1865, in what would be his last public speech, the president repeated his determination to remain flexible regarding Reconstruction and to fashion a liberal and compassionate peace. "So great peculiarities" characterized each of the various Southern states, he said, and "so new and unprecedented" were the problems currently confronting the Union that "no exclusive and inflexible plan" should be adopted at this time.

By now, the war, for all practical purposes, was over. On April 9, Confederate commander Robert E. Lee and the Army of Northern Virginia had surrendered to Grant at Appomattox Court House, Virginia. Lincoln

Lincoln's Second Inaugural Address

The following excerpts are from Lincoln's Second Inaugural Address, delivered on March 4, 1865, a little more than a month before the end of the Civil War. Along with the Gettysburg Address, the Second Inaugural Address is engraved on the walls of the Lincoln Memorial in Washington, D.C.

On the occasion corresponding to this four years ago, all thoughts were anxiously directed to an impending civil-war. All dreaded it— all sought to avert it. . . . Both parties deprecated war; but one of them would *make* war rather than let the nation survive; and the other would *accept* war rather than let it perish. And the war came. . . .

Neither party expected for the war, the magnitude, or the duration, which it has already attained. Neither anticipated that the *cause* of the conflict might cease with, or even before, the conflict itself should cease. Each looked for an easier triumph, and a result less fundamental and astounding. Both read the same Bible, and pray to the same God; and each invokes His aid against the other. . . . The prayers of both could not be answered; that of neither has been answered fully. The Almighty has His own purposes. 'Woe unto the world because of offences! for it must needs be that offences come; but woe to that man by whom the offence cometh!' If we shall suppose therefore believed that the time had come to begin discussing the postwar position of the 4 million slaves who would soon be freed in the South. In his speech on April 11, Lincoln publicly supported voting rights for blacks for the first time, saying that at least literate black Americans or those who had served in the Union army be given the vote immediately. Among those listening to the president's address was a 26-year-old actor and

that American Slavery is one of those offences which, in the providence of God, must needs come, but which, having continued through His appointed time, He now wills to remove, and that He gives to both North and South, this terrible war, as the woe due to those by whom the offence came, shall we discern therein any departure from those divine attributes which the believers in a Living God always ascribe to Him? Fondly do we hope—fervently do we pray—that this mighty scourge of war may speedily pass away. Yet, if God wills that it continue, until all the wealth piled by the bond-man's two hundred and fifty years of unrequited toil shall be sunk, and until every drop of blood drawn with the lash, shall be paid by another drawn with the sword, as was said three thousand years ago, so still it must be said "the judgments of the Lord, are true and righteous altogether."

With malice toward none; with charity for all; with firmness in the right, as God gives us to see the right, let us strive to finish the work we are in; to bind up the nation's wounds; to care for him who shall have borne the battle, and for his widow, and his orphan—to do all which may achieve and cherish a just, and a lasting peace, among ourselves, and with all nations.

white supremacist from Maryland named John Wilkes Booth. Convinced that the United States was "formed for the white, not for the black man," Booth was outraged by Lincoln's talk of granting the vote to freed slaves. "That means nigger citizenship," Booth hissed to a companion, vowing, "That is the last speech he will ever make."

"NOW HE BELONGS TO THE AGES"

On the evening of April 14, 1865 (Good Friday on the Christian calendar), President Lincoln, Mrs. Lincoln, and two guests attended a popular comedic play entitled *Our American Cousin* at Ford's Theater in Washington. At approximately 10:13 P.M., John Wilkes Booth slipped into the president's box, pointed a handgun at the back of Lincoln's head, and fired.

The president lost consciousness immediately. At 7:22 the next morning, Lincoln died, surrounded by family, friends, and all of his cabinet except William Seward, who had been seriously wounded in his home by an accomplice of Booth at about the same time Lincoln was shot. "Now he belongs to the ages," declared Secretary of War Edwin Stanton after the doctors pronounced the 56-year-old president dead.

Never before had a U.S. president been assassinated, and Lincoln's death, coming at the end of a long and terrible civil war in which over 600,000 had died, left Americans profoundly shocked and grief-stricken. The murdered president was given a farewell the likes of

President Lincoln and his wife were enjoying a play at Ford's Theater in Washington, D.C., when John Wilkes Booth sneaked into the president's booth and shot him in the back of the head. Lincoln died the next morning at the age of 56.

which had never been seen before—and has not been seen since—in the history of the Republic. Following a funeral service in the East Room of the White House, Lincoln's body was conveyed in a huge procession to the Capitol, where it lay in state for two days. His casket was then placed on a special funeral train bound for Springfield, Illinois. Elaborate memorial services and processions were held and hundreds of thousands of Americans viewed the slain president's remains in numerous cities along the 1,700-mile route. Finally, on May 4, more than two weeks after the original funeral service at the

Shortly before his assassination, Lincoln recounted a dream he had in which he wandered through a deathly quiet White House: "Then I heard subdued sobs, as if a number of people were weeping." The sound, Lincoln discovered, was coming from the East Room, where he encountered an upsetting sight. "Before me was a catafalque [a structure used in funerals], on which rested a corpse . . . 'Who is dead in the White House?' I demanded of one of the soldiers [standing by the coffin] 'The President,' was his answer, 'he was killed by an assassin!' . . . I slept no more that night . . ."

White House, Abraham Lincoln was laid to rest in Oak Ridge Cemetery in Springfield.

★   ★   ★

When 23-year-old Abraham Lincoln first ran for political office as a candidate for the Illinois legislature, he opened his campaign by declaring, "Every man is said to have his peculiar ambition. . . . I can say for one that I have no other so great as that of being truly esteemed of my fellow men, by rendering myself worthy of their esteem." Few would deny Lincoln's extraordinary success in fulfilling his greatest ambition. Though harshly criticized by his Democratic opponents and even by members of his own party during his presidency, after his assassination, Lincoln was widely praised for his outstanding leadership qualities and high moral character. Today, a century and a half after his death, an estimated 17,000 books about him have been published—far more than have been devoted to any other figure in U.S. history—and presidential scholars typically rank Lincoln as the United States' greatest chief executive. Lincoln's steadfast commitment to preserving the Union, his eloquence, and his basic decency—especially his ability to rise above the hatreds and prejudices caused by the war that consumed his entire presidency—won him the respect of the American people and much of the international community as well. It is easy to believe that no president before or since has been as truly esteemed by his fellow men or, perhaps, has been as worthy of their esteem as Abraham Lincoln.

THE PRESIDENTS OF THE UNITED STATES

George Washington
1789–1797

John Adams
1797–1801

Thomas Jefferson
1801–1809

James Madison
1809–1817

James Monroe
1817–1825

John Quincy Adams
1825–1829

Andrew Jackson
1829–1837

Martin Van Buren
1837–1841

William Henry
Harrison
1841

John Tyler
1841–1845

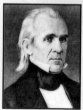

James Polk
1845–1849

Zachary Taylor
1849–1850

Millard Filmore
1850–1853

Franklin Pierce
1853–1857

James Buchanan
1857–1861

Abraham Lincoln
1861–1865

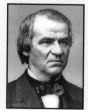

Andrew Johnson
1865–1869

Ulysses S. Grant
1869–1877

Rutherford B. Hayes
1877–1881

James Garfield
1881

Chester Arthur
1881–1885

Grover Cleveland
1885–1889

Benjamin Harrison
1889–1893

Grover Cleveland
1893-1897

William McKinley
1897–1901

Theodore Roosevelt
1901–1909

William H. Taft
1909–1913

Woodrow Wilson
1913–1921

Warren Harding
1921–1923

Calvin Coolidge
1923–1929

Herbert Hoover
1929–1933

Franklin D. Roosevelt 1933–1945

Harry S. Truman
1945–1953

Dwight Eisenhower
1953–1961

John F. Kennedy
1961–1963

Lyndon Johnson
1963–1969

Richard Nixon
1969–1974

Gerald Ford
1974–1977

Jimmy Carter
1977–1981

Ronald Reagan
1981–1989

George H.W. Bush
1989–1993

William J. Clinton
1993–2001

George W. Bush
2001–

Note: Dates indicate years of presidential service.
Source: www.whitehouse.gov

PRESIDENTIAL FACT FILE

THE CONSTITUTION

Article II of the Constitution of the United States outlines several requirements for the president of the United States, including:

* **Age:** The president must be at least 35 years old.

* **Citizenship:** The president must be a U.S. citizen.

* **Residency:** The president must have lived in the United States for at least 14 years.

* **Oath of Office:** On his inauguration, the president takes this oath: "I do solemnly swear (or affirm) that I will faithfully execute the office of President of the United States, and will to the best of my ability, preserve, protect and defend the Constitution of the United States."

* **Term:** A presidential term lasts four years.

PRESIDENTIAL POWERS

The president has many distinct powers as outlined in and interpreted from the Constitution. The president:

* Submits many proposals to Congress for regulatory, social, and economic reforms.

* Appoints federal judges with the Senate's approval.

* Prepares treaties with foreign nations to be approved by the Senate.

* Can veto laws passed by Congress.

* Acts as commander in chief of the military to oversee military strategy and actions.

* Appoints members of the Cabinet and many other agencies and administrations with the Senate's approval.

* Can declare martial law (control of local governments within the country) in times of national crisis.

PRESIDENTIAL FACT FILE

TRADITION

Many parts of the presidency developed out of tradition. The traditions listed below are but a few that are associated with the U.S. presidency.

★ After taking his oath of office, George Washington added, "So help me God." Numerous presidents since Washington have also added this phrase to their oath.

★ Originally, the Constitution limited the term of the presidency to four years, but did not limit the number of terms a president could serve. Presidents, following the precedent set by George Washington, traditionally served only two terms. After Franklin Roosevelt was elected to four terms, however, Congress amended the Constitution to restrict presidents to only two.

★ James Monroe was the first president to have his inauguration outside the Capitol. From his inauguration in 1817 to Jimmy Carter's inauguration in 1977, it was held on the Capitol's east portico. Ronald Reagan broke from this tradition in 1981 when he was inaugurated on the west portico to face his home state, California. Since 1981, all presidential inaugurations have been held on the west portico of the Capitol.

★ Not all presidential traditions are serious, however. One of the more fun activities connected with the presidency began when President William Howard Taft ceremoniously threw out the first pitch of the new baseball season in 1910.  Presidents since Taft have carried on this tradition, including Woodrow Wilson, who is pictured here as he throws the first pitch of the 1916 season. In more recent years, the president has also opened the All-Star and World Series games.

THE WHITE HOUSE

Although George Washington was involved with the planning of the White House, he never lived there. It has been, however, the official residence of every president beginning with John Adams, the second U.S. president. The building was completed approximately in 1800, although it has undergone several renovations since then. It was the first public building constructed in Washington, D.C. The White House has 132 rooms, several of which are open to the public. Private rooms include those for administration and the president's personal residence. For an online tour of the White House and other interesting facts, visit the official White House website, *http://www.whitehouse.gov*.

THE PRESIDENTIAL SEAL

A committee began planning the presidential seal in 1777. It was completed in 1782. The seal appears as an official stamp on medals, stationery, and documents, among other items. Originally, the eagle faced right toward the arrows (a symbol of war) that it held in its talons. In 1945, President Truman had the seal altered so that the eagle's head instead faced left toward the olive branch (a symbol of peace), because he believed the president should be prepared for war but always look toward peace.

PRESIDENT LINCOLN IN PROFILE

PERSONAL

Name: Abraham Lincoln

Birth date: February 12, 1809

Birth place: Hardin County, Kentucky

Father: Thomas Lincoln

Mother: Nancy Hanks Lincoln

Stepmother: Sarah Bush Johnston Lincoln

Wife: Mary Todd Lincoln

Children: Robert, Edward, William, Thomas (Tad)

Death date: April 15, 1865

POLITICAL

Years in office: 1861–1865

Vice president: Hannibal Hamlin (1861–1865); Andrew Johnson (1865)

Occupations before presidency: Lawyer, store owner, state representative

Political party: Republican

Major achievements of presidency: Preserved the Union, issued the Emancipation Proclamation

Nicknames: The Great Emancipator; Honest Abe; Illinois Rail-Splitter

Presidential library:

The Abraham Lincoln Presidential Library
212 N. 6th Street
Springfield, IL 62701

Abraham Lincoln Library and Museum
Lincoln Memorial University
Cumberland Gap Parkway
Harrogate, TN 37752
615/869-6235

The Lincoln Museum
200 E. Berry
P.O. Box 7838
Fort Wayne, IN 46801-7838

Tributes:

The Lincoln Memorial
   (Washington, D.C.; *http://www.nps.gov/linc*);

The Lincoln Memorial Shrine
   (Redlands, CA; *http://www.lincolnshrine.org*);

Lincoln Memorial Garden
   (Springfield, IL; *http://www.lmgnc.com*)

1809   Lincoln is born in a log cabin in Hardin County, Kentucky on February 12.

1816   The Lincoln family moves to Indiana.

1818   Nancy Hanks Lincoln dies.

1819   Thomas Lincoln marries Sarah Bush Johnston.

1830   The Lincoln family moves to Illinois.

1832   Lincoln serves in the Black Hawk War and runs unsuccessfully for the Illinois State Legislature.

1834–42   Lincoln serves in the Illinois House of Representatives as a Whig.

1837   Lincoln settles in Springfield, Illinois, and begins practicing law.

1842   Lincoln marries Mary Todd.

1847–49   Lincoln serves one term in the U.S. Congress as a Whig.

1854   The Kansas–Nebraska Act passes Congress under the leadership of Stephen A. Douglas.

1856   Lincoln leaves the Whig Party and joins the new Republican Party.

1858   The highly publicized Lincoln–Douglas debates during Lincoln's unsuccessful bid for a U.S. Senate seat earn him a national reputation.

1860   Lincoln wins the presidential election, defeating Douglas and three other candidates.

1861

March 4   Lincoln is inaugurated as the 16th president of the United States.

April 12   The Civil War begins with the Confederate attack on Fort Sumter.

July 21   Union troops are defeated at the First Battle of Bull Run, the first major battle of the war.

CHRONOLOGY

1862

September 22   Lincoln issues the Preliminary Emancipation Proclamation five days after the Union victory at Antietam, Maryland.

1863

January 1   Lincoln issues the final Emancipation Proclamation.

July   Union wins victories at Gettsyburg, Pennsylvania, and at Vicksburg, Mississippi.

November   Lincoln delivers his celebrated Gettysburg Address.

1864

March   Lincoln appoints Ulysses S. Grant as general in chief of the Union armies.

September   William Tecumseh Sherman takes Atlanta.

November   Lincoln is reelected, defeating Democrat George McClellan.

1865

January   The Thirteenth Amendment passes Congress, abolishing slavery in the United States.

March 4   Lincoln is inaugurated for a second term as president.

April 9   Lee surrenders the Army of Northern Virginia to Grant at Appomattox Court House.

April 14   Lincoln is shot by John Wilkes Booth at Ford's Theater in Washington, D.C.

April 15   Lincoln dies at 7:22 A.M.

BIBLIOGRAPHY

Axelrod, Alan. *The Civil War.* New York: Macmillan, 1998.

Catton, Bruce. *The Civil War.* New York: American Heritage, 1960.

Donald, David Herbert. *Lincoln.* New York: Simon and Schuster, 1995.

Donald, David Herbert. *Lincoln at Home: Two Glimpses of Abraham Lincoln's Family Life.* New York: Simon and Schuster, 1999.

Fehrenbacher, Don E., ed. *The Leadership of Abraham Lincoln.* New York: John Wiley, 1970.

Foner, Eric. "Was Abraham Lincoln a Racist?" *The Los Angeles Times.* April 9, 2000.

Gienapp, William E. *Abraham Lincoln and Civil War America: A Biography.* New York: Oxford University Press, 2002.

Gienapp, William E., ed. *The Fiery Trail: The Speeches and Writings of Abraham Lincoln.* New York: Oxford University Press, 2002.

Kunhardt, Philip B., Jr., Philip B. Kunhardt III, and Peter W. Kunhardt. *Lincoln: An Illustrated Biography.* New York: Alfred A. Knopf, 1992.

Miller, William Lee. *Lincoln's Virtues: An Ethical Biography.* New York: Alfred A. Knopf, 2002.

Neely, Mark E., Jr. *The Last Best Hope of Earth: Abraham Lincoln and the Promise of America.* Cambridge, Mass.: Harvard University Press, 1993.

Neely, Mark E., Jr., ed. *The Abraham Lincoln Encyclopedia.* New York: McGraw-Hill, 1982.

Paludan, Phillip S. *The Presidency of Abraham Lincoln.* Lawrence, Kan.: University Press of Kansas, 1994.

Thomas, Benjamin P. *Abraham Lincoln: A Biography.* New York: Alfred A. Knopf, 1952.

White, Ronald C. *Lincoln's Greatest Speech: The Second Inaugural.* New York: Simon and Schuster, 2002.

Bibliography

WEBSITES

Abraham Lincoln Online
   http://www.netins.net/showcase/creative/lincoln.html

Britannica Online Encyclopedia, 2001, "Abraham Lincoln."
   http://www.britannica.com

FURTHER READING

Burchard, Peter. *Lincoln and Slavery.* New York: Atheneum, 1999.

Cothran, Helen, ed. *Abraham Lincoln.* San Diego: Greenhaven Press, 2002.

Freedman, Russell. *Lincoln: A Photobiography.* New York: Clarion Books, 1987.

Holzer, Harold. *Abraham Lincoln the Writer: A Treasury of His Greatest Speeches and Letters.* Honesdale, Penn.: Boyds Mill Press, 2000.

Kunhardt, Philip B., Jr., Philip B. Kunhardt III, and Peter W. Kunhardt. *Lincoln: An Illustrated Biography.* New York: Alfred A. Knopf, 1992.

Marrin, Albert. *Commander in Chief: Abraham Lincoln and the Civil War.* New York: Dutton Children's Books, 1997.

Neely, Mark E., Jr., ed. *The Abraham Lincoln Encyclopedia.* New York: McGraw-Hill, 1982.

WEBSITES

Abraham Lincoln Online
http://www.netins.net/showcase/creative/lincoln.html

Abraham Lincoln Research Site
http://members.aol.com/RVSNorton/Lincoln2.html

Lincoln's Virtual Library:
The Abraham Lincoln Papers at the Library of Congress
http://lcweb2.loc.gov/ammem/alhtml/alhome.html

INDEX

INDEX

INDEX

INDEX

PICTURE CREDITS

page:

11: The Lincoln Museum, Ft. Wayne, Indiana
17: The Abraham Lincoln Library and
    Museum, Lincoln Memorial University,
    Harrogate, Tennessee
21: Courtesy of the Illinois State Historical
    Library
30: Library of Congress
31: Library of Congress
33: Library of Congress
37: Library of Congress
43: Library of Congress
47: Courtesy The National Park Service
48: Library of Congress

48: Library of Congress
51: Library of Congress
53: Courtesy The National Park Service
56: © Bettmann/CORBIS
59: Library of Congress
69: Library of Congress
74: Courtesy The National Park Service
77: Library of Congress
83: Library of Congress
84: The Lincoln Museum, Ft. Wayne, Indiana
86-87: Courtesy Library of Congress,
    "Portraits of the Presidents and First
    Ladies" American Memory Collection

Cover: Library of Congress

ACKNOWLEDGMENTS

Thank you to Celebrity Speakers Intl. for coordinating Mr. Cronkite's
contribution to this book.

Louise Chipley Slavicek received her master's degree in history from the University of Connecticut. She has written many articles on historical topics for young people's magazines and is the author of six other books for young people, including *Women of the Revolutionary War*, *Israel*, and *Juan Ponce de León*. She lives in Ohio with her husband, Jim, a research biologist, and their two children, Krista and Nathan.

Walter Cronkite has covered virtually every major news event during his more than 60 years in journalism, during which he earned a reputation for being "the most trusted man in America." He began his career as a reporter for the United Press during World War II, taking part in the beachhead assaults of Normandy and covering the Nuremberg trials. He then joined *CBS News* in Washington, D.C., where he was the news anchor for political convention and election coverage from 1952 to 1980. CBS debuted its first half-hour weeknight news program with Mr. Cronkite's interview of President John F. Kennedy in 1963. Mr. Cronkite was inducted into the Academy of Television Arts and Sciences in 1985 and has written several books. He lives in New York City with his wife of 59 years.